“The Ups The Downs The Tweens”

By Meghan Chatfield

This collection of poems is a glimpse inside of a bipolar mind. Some of these poems are dark and contain difficult content; if you will find this triggering, I kindly ask you to refrain from reading. I dedicate this book to all of the wonderful people who have helped me, and continue to help me, on my journey: friends, family, doctors, nurses, therapist, techs, coworkers and fellow patients.

Special Thanks: Maggie Crescentini, Tanya Taylor,

Amy Buchanan, and the Hendley Family

<u>Acrostics</u>

Broken

Unstable

Revolting

Damaged

Emotional

Neurotic

  Burden

  Repulsive

  Obese

  Krazy

  Erratic

  Nervous

    Persistent

    Agony

    In

    Nerves

Temperamental

Inconsolable

Retched

Evil

Depressed

Sensitive

Injured

Callous

Kinder

Appealing

Needling

Guttural

Exciting

Relieving

Hurt

Cut away the pain

Scratch away the hurt

Pinch away the nerves

Gnaw away the fear

Just a little knife

Just a little blood

Just a little peace is all I need

Reminisce

Blood, I miss blood

Pain lingers, cuts sting

Scratches bleed, must stop

Words of childhood

Smack

Bang

Crash

Slam

Yell

Scream

Dodge

Break

Sneak

Sin

Cut

Scratch

Cry

Wretch

Choke

Scrub

Watch

Wait

Wail

Young One

Little child, little child

Why do you cry so?

Little child, little child

I am here to console.

Little child, little child

Oh the troubles you have seen.

Little child, little child

That is simply what has been.

Little child, little child

Dry your sorrowful tears.

Little child, little child

Not to worry, I am here.

Little child, little child

You don't have to hurt anymore

Little child, little child

Comfort has come to your door.

Summer Fades

Green leaves, swaying trees

Feel the grass beneath your feet

Buzzing bees, gentle breeze

Watermelon, so good to eat

Feel the sun upon your brow

Summer is coming to and end now

Fireworks, party bags

Last bash of summer

Sand pits, punching bags

Back to school, what a bummer

Summer ends

Fall begins

Hospital

Stuck again, nowhere to run

White coats, blue scrubs

Medicine window, cafeteria food

Hard beds, foam doors

Not sure I can take much more

Storm

Pitter pat on the window pane

Winds whistle through the trees

A lull to sleep begins

Crack! Lighting flashes through the sky

Boom! Thunder crashes in the night

The pitter pat becomes a din

An evening storm has begun

The small child awakes with a start

The branches bang against the window frame

Running down the hall, seeking refuge

A warm bed, two sets of grown up feet

Lift the covers and burrow under

Safe from the danger, finding comfort

The adults roll over, not surprised to find the sleeping child.

A kiss to the foreheads, a nuzzle to the stomach, a tickle on the toes.

What once was two became three,

And now they all have sweet dreams.

The C word

Cancer, a big word

Cancer, a scary word

Cancer, an endless battle

Cancer, one hell of a fight

Cancer, one heck of a competitor

Cancer, one treatment at a time

Cancer, doesn't have to win

Cancer, doesn't have to mean death

Cancer, doesn't mean life is over

Cancer, can be beaten

Caner, will change your life forever

Cancer, can give you new purpose

Calm

Arising from sleep

The mind is at peace

A tired body

But a quiet head

No sense of fear or agitation

No frightening things scaring the imagination

Anxiety is a thing of the past

Fearfulness doesn't seem to last

The kind relief is welcome

Winter's Delight

Cold, glistening night
Cool, shimmering days

Coat, gloves, hat
Sweater, warm underwear

Shinning, white delight

Soup, chili, cider
Hot coco, warm tea

A wonderland of delight
A beautiful sight

A winter's pleasant aroma

Ups and Downs

Flying high one day

Drowning the next

Thrilling to survive

Longing to die

The Competition

Standing on the edge
Shaking with anticipation
Legs shake, arms swing
Head covered, heart pounding
Warm sun beating down
Sunscreen applied, goggles on
A deep breath, shot fires
Dive in, what a splash
Stroke hard, holding breath
Breathe, turn, repeat
Reach the wall, first place
What a race, swimming with delight

Springtime Bliss

Honeysuckle in the air

Blossoms blooming everywhere

Bunnies hop, ducklings waddle

Birds chirp, mothers swaddles

Cool grass, warm sun

Springtime has begun

The flower's sweet aroma

All senses heightened

A lovely spring day

Not a care in your way

Lost and Losing

Life if not fair or just

Illness wrecks havoc

Lives spent, lies spread

Sickness touches everyone

Father, Mother, Sister, Brother

Plagued my mind and body

Death threatens life

Prostate, Breast, Gun

One Dying

One Fighting

One Dead

I have no control

Cards

Smooth, slick paper

Red, black, and white

Number duce through ace

Pick up one, place down another

Runs and sets

Poking fun and light insults

Young and old around the table

All are welcome, if you're able

Come sit down, pull up a chair

Everyone plays everywhere

Falling

And down goes the hope

Down goes the happiness

Quick like a switch

Sudden like a crash

The spiral downward has begun

I wouldn't wish the hell on anyone

Words of marriage

SMACK

freeze

SCREAM

flinch

BANG

cringe

BONG

cover

HIT

flight

HAMMER

Fright

Fight

Survive

Damaged Goods

Raped, how did I get here?

Ravaged, why did I get here?

Wrecked, when did I get here?

Destroyed, where am I?

Demolished, who am I?

Bruised, what am I?

Abused

A little phrase said too loud

"Shut the fuck up!"

Brings me back to where I used to be

"Shut the fuck up."

Cuts, bruises, fractured bone, and sprained ligaments

"Shut. The. Fuck. Up."

Damaged feelings, wounded pride

"Shut the fuck up!"

Ego shattered, burned face

"Shut the fuck up"

Happy memories erased

Coping Skill

Rubber bands snaps

Relief comes

Pain that won't leave a scar

Appropriate pain, that isn't harmful

All the pain, none of the blood

It nearly does the trick

Booze

A sweet release each sip

A warm sensation against your lip

A tasty buzz upon your tongue

A hot sensation down your throat

A full feeling in your belly

A dizziness in your head

A numbness in your limbs

A drink enjoyed morning, noon, and night

Peter Pan Syndrome

Always a child

Stuck at sixteen

Putting on a happy face

MCR, my go to jams

Rock out to space out

Growth stunted, needs never met

Desperately seeking affirmation

Starved for love, touch deprives

Breaking out in tears for no reason

Begging for hugs, given strange looks

Will I ever learn to love me?

Will I ever grow up?

Joyful

Friendship, laughter all around

Frivolity, smiling faces and happy places

Footloose and fancy free

Peaceful, kindness abounds

Pacify, soothing words

Pensive, thoughtfulness and joy

Summer Days

A warm breeze

A cool stream

A leaning tree

A tire swing

A glass o' lemonade

How sweetly pass th hours

A setting sun

Day is done

A rising moon

Comes too soon

A cool breeze

A warm stream

A leaning tree

A tire swing

How slowly pass the hours

A setting moon

The night is through

A rising sun

Fun has begun

Snowfall

Snowflakes fall on a quiet night
The moon gleams bright on a bed a white
Fresh flakes so sharp and pristine
A newly covered hill oh so clean

The sun begins to rise, shinning bright
Snowflake fly off into the night
A child awakes filled with delight
Giddy with joy at the snow covered sight

A large silver sled, so round and light
Warm woolen mittens, and a jacket zipped tight
Down the hill he goes shouting "All right!"
Fresh tracks on the fresh snow shine bright

As the child plays late into the day
The sun begins to set and it's time to go away
Up the hill he treads back home and all
And as he turns to say goodbye a snowflake falls

Fall's splendor

Red, yellow, brown
Leaves rustle around
Apples cider, pumpkin spice
A warm drink is nice

Barren trees, lovely leaves
Apple picking, corn mazes
Pumpkin patches, haunted houses
Strolling through the woods

Carnivals and carousels
Child running free
Bonfires and smores
Crisp breeze, cool night

Oh how lovely is fall's delight

Resource

Abandoned again.

Made to feel like less than.

Left behind, discarded

Maybe I'll stop caring.

Maybe I'll show you.

Maybe I'll win and make you regret it, give you more guilt.

Maybe you deserve it, maybe it is your fault.

I didn't use you, but you sure made it seem like it.

Maybe I'll just die, then what will you have to say?

Death by IT

If I hit enough funny faces maybe I'll laugh.

If I hit enough hearts maybe mine will heal.

If I hit enough likes, maybe I'll like myself.

Watch enough videos, read enough articles,

Dive into the digital world to forget about my own.

Crime dramas and reality shows,

Drown in false tv instead of my own misery.

<u>Deathwish</u>

Sometimes I feel like dying would be less painful.

At times, the idea of never waking up again is what leads me to sleep.

I try to remind myself the pain I'd leave behind, but sometimes it pales in comparison.

I try to think of the imposition I'd be placing on others, but everybody has to die sometime.

I try to think of those that would be hurt, but sometimes I feel my existence hurts them more.

I try to think of those that wouldn't understand, and I wish I could explain.

Sometimes when i wish i may i wish i might, the wish i make is to die tonight.

Why not

No one would miss me, not for long

No one needs me now

My job can hire someone else

Those that love me will move on

I'm fat, ugly, troubled, stupid, and worthless

It'd be better for everyone to stop the misery

The only thing stopping me is the fear of making others angry,

but they'd forgive me because I'd stop feeling terrible

I'd stop needing help

I'd stop being an imposition

I'd stop leaving folks on pins and needles

Desire

Cut, scratch, bleed

Eat, choke, vomit

Puff, puff, and puff again

Addiction at its simplest

Bleed, bleed, bled

Vomit, choke, vomit

Puff, puff and puff again

Addiction at its best

Bleeding, blackout

Vomit, bleed

Puff, puff, choke

Addiction at its worst

cut, choke, puff

cut, choke, puff

Till you can't no more

Addiction wants to win

Battered by every force

No one answers when I call

No one answers when I pray

I speak and no one hears me

I cry and no one knows

I bleed and no one sees

I might as well be no one

Rage

Like a monster crawling from the deep,

Anger seething through me.

Feelings of disgust and injustice,

Anger invades my very soul.

I want to kick and scream and shout,

Anger envelopes my spirit.

I want to punch things and break things,

Anger begging for release from within me.

Annoyance

I'm sorry I'm difficult

I'm sorry I can be obtuse

I'm sorry I self-sabotage

I'm sorry I self-mutilate

I'm sorry I can't always choose good

I'm sorry I'm a failure

I'm sorry I'm an annoyance

Fun

I laughed,

I joked,

I cuddled,

I hugged,

I snuggled,

I booped,

I watch children have innocent fun.

I talked,

I cheered,

I booed,

I ate yummy food.

I listened to music and danced and sang along.

I didn't think about drugging or cutting or vomiting.

I just had pure unadulterated fun.

I felt loved and cherished and cared for.

Munchkin is sorry

I'm sorry I'm needy

I'm sorry I'm bad

I'm sorry I'm hurt

I'm sorry I'm naughty

I'm sorry I'm chubby

I'm sorry I'm a hand full

I'm sorry I'm too determined

I'm sorry I'm not good enough

I'm sorry I made you leave

I'm sorry I made you hurt me

I'm sorry I misbehaved

I'm sorry I'm dirty

I'm sorry I whine

I'm sorry I'm a bad girl

Fine red line

Drip, drop my troubles seem to melt away

Scritch, scratch the bliss of pain A weapon grasped firm within my hand Dare I cut more, cut deeper?

A small reprieve from the chaos in my mind

The blood trickles down my arm

I think, if I just press a little harder, if I just cut a different angle

Then again no

I'm not in a tub, it would be quite a mess

I'm sitting in a chair, at a computer, at a school

Snap back to reality, no one can see me like this

Hide the evidence, wipe of the blood, plaster on the smile and pretend you're fine

Would it be so bad

If I died? The pain would end for me

If I died? I wouldn’t be a burden anymore

If I died? They could hire someone new

If I died? Those who care would recover

If I died? I wouldn’t care about those who don't

If I died? I'd see my loved ones in heaven

If I died? The world would stop hurting

Damaged goods 2

Soiled, imperfect, blemished, marred, Screwed up.

Flawed, bruised, discarded, disgusting, Mucked up.

Worthless, helpless, hideous, loveless, Loused up.

Hidden, ignored, beaten, defiled, Fucked up.

Melancholy

It's times like these I wonder if I'm going crazy.

One minute I'm sad beyond all measure, the next I feel alright,

Sometimes even elated, but the high never lasts.

Sometimes I miss the spells, the feeling like I'd never fall back to earth.

In these moments I think maybe I should stop my meds

But I know that's a bad idea because highs come with lows.

Mostly I think how unfair it all is.

Child

It was not your fault

It is not your fault

It will never be your fault

You deserved love

You deserve love

You will always deserve love

You deserved protection

You deserve protection

You will be protected

I am sorry no one was there for you

I am here for you now

It is not your fault

You are safe

You are loved

You are wanted

It is not your fault

No will to live

I should be working on my journal

I should be doing laundry

I should be putting the groceries away

I should be taking a shower

I should be working on my audition piece

I should be cleaning the house

Instead I'm stuck here on the couch incapacitated by my crushing depression.

Wishes

I wish I felt unconditionally loved by my family

I wish I felt like I could be honest with people

I wish I liked work

I wish I cared about my house

I wish I cared about my health

I wish I cared about my life

I wish I could die

I wish I could take my life

Mean to myself

I expect too much, I crave perfection

I try to control my feelings

I wallow in dread but never float in ecstasy

I binge and purge, and purge, and don't eat

I pick on myself for needing meds

I take sharp implements to my skin

I don't think I'm beautiful

I call myself names

I believe I am worthless

I believe I'm a whore

Downward

And just like that joy turns to sorrow

And just like that love turns to loneliness

And just like that satiated turns to starving

And just like that cherished turns to ignored

And just like that cuddled turns to cold

Let me down easy

Tell me the truth, I'm difficult

Tell me straight, I'm a mess

Give it to me I can take it, I'm too broken

Don't hold back, I'm not worthy of your love

I think I love you

I know that I love you, I just don't know how.

In some ways you're like a mother to me, in other ways a friend, and yet again like a confidant.

It baffles my brain how you can be so many wonderful things in one.

Sometimes I want to hug you until all the hurt goes away, my head nestled on you like a child.

Sometimes I want to laugh away the day with you like two old friends.

Sometimes I want to cuddle, safe in your loving arms.

Most of the time I want to do all three.

I think it's because you're the first person I've ever been truly open and honest with.

I think it's because you make me feel safe.

I do know this, you're the only person to ever make me feel loved unconditionally.

Hurting again

Dying inside, scared to go back to the world I knew.

Wishing everyone would just go away so I could slip into the vast chasm of despair a

wallow there until there is no more air

choking on alibis and sad goodbyes wondering

all the while why no one dries my swollen eyes

I want to take a blade to all the parts of my untouched flesh,

I want to drink until the room spins,

I want to smoke till I touch the sky,

Someone save me,

I'm calling out in to the dark lifeless void where the monsters lurk to love me.

Tic-toc

The cold drink in my right hand
The cool bottle in my left
Contemplation Consternation

The cold drink in my left hand
The plastic bottle in my right
Complacent Compliant

So afraid, so ready
So annoyed, so inept

Planning Woes

I don't think I can do this
I don't think I'm ready for a new school year
I don't think I'm a good enough teacher
I could barely get my room ready, & I cried
I told everyone I was great, but it was a lie
I told everyone I had a good summer, but that's only part true
I plastered a smile on most of the day and it hurt
I'm not sure how long I can fake it
I'm even less sure how much I can take it

You don’t know

Do you know what it's like to wake up every day wishing you hadn't?

Do you know what it's like to wish that you were dead, more often than not?

Do you know what it's like to want to get drunk all the time?

Do you know what it's like to do all the things you're supposed to and still feel miserable?

Do you know what it's like to suffer for no known reason?

Do you know what it's like to want to take your life?

Free to be Frightened

Every little thing that goes bump in the night fills me with dread.

Every flash of light makes me think I'm dead.

Every unexpected touch makes me want to fight.

Every unexpected sound fills me with fright.

I can't shower enough to wash you off of me,

I can't shower too much or I think of how you hurt me.

Neglected, rejected, and yet somehow you own me.

Death's erotic melody

Calling ever sweetly
Singing so seductively
Humming with reckless abandon
Drumming
passionately
Serenading
exotically

I dance along to the music
I clap along to beat
I sing along
to the words
I want to
dive so deep
into his spell
To hear him croon,
that tune I know so well.

Listen to me

I want to play and frolic
I want to dance and sing
I want to color and laugh
I want to be held with a loving touch
I want someone to notice the hurt
I want someone to stop the pain
I want to be a tomboy
I want to dress up
I want to be listened to
I want to be noticed
I want to matter
I want you to acknowledge how smart I am
I want you to love me
I want you to accept me
I want you to stop shunning me
I want you to protect me

Scrubbed

Raw scratching against my skin
Putrid smell reaches my nostril
Burning sensation in my pores
Nails pull against my innards
Between my toes, up my thighs
Between my fingers, on my chest
No no not there, anywhere but there
Bleached from head to toe, inside and out
No more dirty girl, no more naughty child
Don't tell anyone or it'll happen again

Alone

No one understands quite MY pain
No one understands quite MY sadness
No one understands quite MY problems
Some make a valiant effort, but they aren't inside my head
Its times like these I wonder, why am I so alone?

Sadness

Crying again, angry and hurt
Crying again, flashbacks
Crying again, body aches
Crying again, feeling dirty
Crying again, feeling naughty Crying again, feeling unloved

Why

Why do you hate me?
Why do you doubt me?
Why do you berate me?
Why can't you stand the sight of me?
Why didn't you protect me?
Why don't you love me?

My sweet friend

She is always there for me.
She is always comforting.
She is always precise.
Usually cold, she can be warmed.
She cleans up easily, but always leaves her mark.
She shines like silver, she's sturdy like wood.
Some see her as a simple tool, but she's more precious to me.
Meet my friend, blade.

Wanting Better

I want better for myself...
I want to be healthy, mentally and physically.
To be happy and peaceful.
To be able to resist temptation.
To not be obsessed with my addictions.
To find faith.
To cement friendship.
To forgive.
To love myself unconditionally.
To be joyous.

<u>Dear one</u>

My dear one it was not yours, is not yours, will not be your fault
My dear one despite the faults of others you are loved and cherished.
My dear one I'm sorry I wasn't there for you, I will be now.
My dear one you are not to blame, you are not bad.
My dear one you are an innocent child who should be embraced with kindness.
I will be that embrace, that love, that kindness, I will cherish you.

<u>Don’t beat yourself up</u>

You didn't drown, you survived
You don't have to be the dart board
I’m getting better, whether or not you like it
the glass is half full, but I'm getting there
Take the risk, work your way to deliverance
Work a purpose because you want better
You're going to make it, cause your making it
There's more new in front of us, than old behind us;
you're worth finding out what the new is
Look for the truth and find a solution

Little Girl

You are just a little girl, you are not to blame
You are just a little girl, you did nothing wrong
You are just a little girl, it is not your fault.
You are just a little girl who needs protection and compassion.
You are just a little girl who needs love and comfort.
You are just a little girl.

Notice me

I'm screaming from the shadows trying to break free, why wont you notice me?
I'm shouting from the rooftops how much I love you, why won't you love me?
I come out at night, when your guard is down, and still you stifle me?
Stop hurting me, stop ignoring me.
How many times do I need to dye your hair crazy colors?
How many cool dresses do I need to buy?
How messy do things have to be before you'll give me the time of day?
Don't you think I was shunned, hurt, and ignored long enough?
Enough is enough, stop ignoring me.

Myself again

What even is myself?
I don't think I want to feel like me again
I want to feel like a new person
A person who is strong and powerful
A person who is courageous and bold
A person who is happy and healthy
Myself again?
No thanks, I'll take better

Urge to cry

I can't shake this urge to cry,
but the tears won't come.
I can't shake this urge to die,
but death won't visit me.
I feel enshrouded by doom
I feel exhausted by life.

Here it comes again

Black, choking, hazy, overwhelming

Grey, stifling, foggy, overbearing

A thick cloud of doom

A loud boom of destruction

So long it stayed away, or at least it seemed

So long it didn't stumble on the scene

Now I crumble and cringe

I cry out for mercy but there is none

I want to run and hide, but it finds me

I want to scream, but it strangles me

I want to bleed myself dry and not feel pain

I want the nightmares to end

Too much and not enough

Too fat

Too lazy

Too opinionated

Too talkative

Too fragile

Too sick

Too needy

Too selfish

Too reckless

Too much to handle

Not skinny enough

Not feminine enough

Not strong enough

Not athletic enough

Not christian enough

Not patriotic enough

Not wealthy enough

Not attentive enough

Not happy enough

Not funny enough

Loneliness

I don't like to be alone.

I thought I did, because I like quiet time, but I don't.

I can not be alone with my thoughts, its dangerous.

I need something or someone to fill the void.

I don't need crowds or noise, but I need company.

I need company I can trust.

I need company that makes me feel good about myself.

I don't like to be alone.

Sick

Sometimes I wonder if my body gets sick because my mind is sick.

Sometimes I wonder if someone as sickly as me deserves to live.

Sometimes I wonder if people get annoyed of how sick I always am.

Sometimes I wonder if people would understand why I said enough.

Sometimes I wonder what it would be like to die and be sick no more.

People think

People love me, why can't I love myself

People think I'm pretty, why don't I see it

People think I'm funny, why can't I laugh

People think I'm courageous, why am I full of fear

People think I'm friendly, why do I feel so awkward

People think I'm kind, why do I feel so judgmental

People think I'm strong, why do I feel so weak

People think I've got this, I've got nothing

Reality Checklist

I am smart

I am kind

I am loving

I am compassionate

I am caring

I am loved

I am wanted

I am beautiful

I am good

Righteous Anger

3 years they've had his computer,

3 years we thought they were working a case,

3 years we waited for justice, and now nothing will be done.

Dropped, the fucking case is dropped, as if it doesn't matter.

Dropped this his casket in the ground.

Dropped, like my fucking mental health.

I'm angry, no pissed, no explanation just dropped.

Bryce deserves more, he deserves justice.

We deserve more, those bastards should rot in jail for what they did.

Fuck the system, it kills the innocent and abandons the needy.

Enough

I am enough.

I am good.

I am kind.

I am loving.

I am loved.

I am enough.

www.ingramcontent.com/pod-product-compliance
Lightning Source LLC
LaVergne TN
LVHW041233150826
845673LV00008B/2379
9798746389343